Who Owns What Here?

Who Owns What Here?

Poems by

Shenan Hahn

Cover by Shay Culligan
Cover art by Shenan Hahn

ISBN: 978-1-63980-104-6

Kelsay Books
502 South 1040 East, A-119
American Fork, Utah 84003
Kelsaybooks.com

To Chris—

who found me halfway through these adventures—

and traveled with me.

Acknowledgments

The following pieces first appeared in print or online:

Softblow: “CAUTION:,” “Remainder,” “Rivers,” “Thor’s Well”

Rust + Moth: “Omens”

The Inflectionist Review: “The Call,” “Marrow”

formercactus: “The Rockabilly Queen of Alaska”

Riggwelter: “We Daughters”

Eunoia Review: “Murder Ballads,” “The Runoff and the Rain”

Contents

We Daughters

We of strange lullabies, we women
with bare skin and splinters,
we with long hair wrangled into brush piles
that we carry on our shoulders, we who tend
to the growth outside ourselves
that we can't see by day, by day,
only by the years that have fallen
around us, we with short edges
sheared over a sink
who can't be bothered to keep anything
that doesn't serve us.
We daughters wrapped in fathers' wool,
starched stiff by a wind that hasn't stopped blowing
since before we got here, warm but not soft,
we who smell like smoke, like spearmint.
We who first knew love as water,
we river girls, we with snail shells in our feet,
we who let our heads go under
to see what drowning might feel like,
we who got carried away,
rotted rubber under our nails
holding tight to tire's edge,
whipping through whitewater thinking we could
but not sure we wanted
to step off, to find our footing,
we who felt the chill of getting out, of leaving,

gripping our own bodies as we were left in turn,
as water evaporated off our skin, shooting into the sky
as if we'd never slowed our blood to show it
how we really could belong
there,
how we could stay forever, weightless
tadpoles in its sway.
We who learned to seek out slate in the sun.
We who learned to bend our bones like stalks of corn,
to grow toward different lights.
Our tongues were torches.
Our feet were moths.
We who were raised under kitchen tables,
fed our mothers' words by scrap and spoonful,
nourished by boasts of changing a car tire
as deftly as one makes peanut pie.
We who gather hungry by the roadside now,
insist on walking.
Our feet are flares.
Our hands are holding fast
to our own bodies.

The Runoff and the Rain

It was the year you never stayed
in one town for longer than to lay bait,
be hooked through the mouth a little,
the year I moved north to the peninsula,
tried waiting
for someone to come home,
planted myself
in a rented room above a small-town bar.

It was after the spring we drank straight from the bottle
in the hills under cover
of fir needles and alder bark falling dry
from a rainless winter
and you said you wanted to leave, and I wondered if I shouldn't
want a seat saved for me somewhere,
when we were both too polite not to
give our numbers to a man lying about wanting our help
writing letters to his landlord, when we listened
to his voicemails we'd never return
all summer we sat bare shoulder to bare shoulder
to bare shoulder damn near every night,
damn the morning, tried to understand
force and angle at the end of a pool stick,
knowing the scatter would always surprise us
like dry heat cracking before a storm.

It was between the time you told me
about the first jump you made
into a car of strangers
and the time I split the head of my first halibut with gaff,
tried to feel its fear and thank it
with its blood misting my boots
on a dock miles from where I'd wanted
to be a regular with someone,

because I wondered why I shouldn't,
if I could,
why it should be as easy
as that.

There we lay in the dark, in the in-between,
when I'd just moved in,
me on the bed, you on the couch,
the jukebox still pulsing through the floorboards
below us. Our confessions floated like a fog
distilling in the night, and with each one we wondered
how we went on after,
and went on after,
how it could be so simple later as to not have happened,
wondered if our happiness would ever balance
the equation of how much pain we sow, if any
thing wrung from us
could outweigh the others.

In the morning it must have been warm enough
that you didn't notice you left your coat.
Not knowing it was yours or where it came from,
I wore it every day that winter,
a little too tight on the top button.
You told me that you'd made your peace with losing it
the next time you saw me, that it was mine by then,
whose was it, really,
when we can suit ourselves to so much, and did

that year we learned that the earth doesn't quake
and crumble from our sins but sweeps them into the water
with everything else, the mud, the blood,

the runoff to the rain and rain again,
wondering what kind of place that made this,
if we too could be swept away
that easy.

The Call

There is a bird that sounds like a child / wailing / a trapped thing /
an SOS / it comes from the trees / behind you / makes you snap
your head / walk and walk / until it doesn't follow
you anymore / you're out of range / I only have dreams
where you're alive / you've gone to live /
in a neighbor's basement / and I coax you home / I dream
my dreams / are signs / that you're near / I gather them like stones
in a pile / when I can't see you / when you're like a sound
deafening
on this bay / I found / a jaw with teeth like tack boxes /
in a row / bone white pestles /
I pocketed it / I want to hold / something
that could have overtaken / me / I want that cry to be
your call / as long as I can't place it / it could be /
we want to hear / the world talking to us / in this place /
among places / we'll hear our names
in any unfinished song / a warble from a rusty saw that rises /
and rains back down / in rivulets / soft and terrible /
a voice so familiar /
it hurts / to listen.

No One Lives Outside (Sestina)

Most of what we call "omens"
is just what we fear, already happening
to someone else - vultures with faces
like masks circling a snuffed out life
on the road we walk, a rabbit screaming
from the trees out of view. We hear our own voice.

The world speaks in a chattering of voices,
a radio show familiar and far away, everyone's omens
crossing into uncanny static, whispering
that our bodies are not our own to hold sacred: what happens
here happens to all of us. Life
in this town does not distinguish faces.

My dog runs toward danger. He faces
the woods, tail straight like an antenna, losing my voice
to the call of a life
he once lived, familiar and far away, an omen
of what could happen
if he doesn't kill what kills, stop the shrieking

he can't see, the crying
of his cells to fly into the storm, unsure in the face
of all this whether he is predator or prey. Happening
upon the place where they meet -- not in theory, but in a voice
that speaks to us plainly: "This is not an omen.
This just is. No one lives outside this life."

No one lives outside this town, no life
so far removed from the grid that the shouts
of birds can't find them. They portend
a flight pattern we've been studying in our sleep, their faces
perched like checkers around the water tower, their voices
silent for the moment as they watch. What is happening

in this place is not for you, you only happened
to be born here, among the living.
You can raise your voice
and it might reach the water tower, and you might hear it echo,
but you still can't tell from their faces
if they are doctor or plague, which one you are, what omen

cracks from your beak. A whimper
is enough to turn their faces
toward you. Let them take you as a sign.

CAUTION:

The redwoods would have rather
let themselves go up in smoke than evacuate,
heads stubbornly in the oven
as if to say, "Our constancy will stay
unchanged even if the landscape doesn't."
We devote ourselves
where we can.

I ate a sandwich alone on the border
between my state and what was then still yours
and the air was thin and languid
despite EXTREME WILDFIRE DANGER
spelled out in strobing bulbs along the highway.
A man in dirt-rubbed overalls
let his son stuff his turkey club
with too many condiments.
You waited,
acres of old growth still between us.

When I found you, we joked about the bridges
you were burning on your way out,
finger-painted tenuous good omens
from the dunes we didn't find
until just in time to see the sky
going the way of the singeing trees,
running off with itself
to leave us
pulling zippers and hoods in tighter on the beach.
So close the smell of bark cracking in the heat,
the north we couldn't see.

Omen

In a world that burns
our houses indiscriminately, draws
our exit numbers double-blind,
lets us pull ourselves apart like chicken bones,

even love is a slow-gestating time-
bomb in our guts,
grief growing inside us
day by day unseen.
We can't decipher
if what we feel is the rest of us
growing in to caulk our empty spaces,
fed by the new light we're churning in,
or a mass of live wires wrapping around
each part of us we've always trusted
to be there.

I trace your tattoos beneath my eyelids.
Wake suddenly at the smell of your shoulder
so strong it must be your ghost.
Cradle an egg in my fingers,
convinced it's heavier than the rest,
terrified an embryo—slick with feathers,
eyes clouded in aborted opening,
tongue snapped shut—
will tumble out.
Stab it with a pair of scissors
probing, and probing, until
shattering, decimating the shell
to shrapnel.

A yellow yolk slides out among the wreckage
bright as day.

Remainder

Take this ridge, you said,
and I did, the farms on one side,
the town and the college below
on the other, the one where you'd idle your car
to kiss berry-basted lips
years before you could have spotted me from there.
Take this, the Super 8 where you worked
in high school, would sneak your friends into
rooms, this the reservoir and the water tower
where you jumped, your father's
balcony where you'd smoke cigarettes,
your friend's house in the hills
where you got snowed in one winter
and felt a cold sting you didn't have a name for
yet.

I've tried to tell you
how I'm always more homesick
for other people's past lives than mine,
how they burrow into me
and pulse like an ember shook loose
from a butt you flicked away,
smoldering still without your breath,
the heat of your car hood
after you've shut off the engine.

When I led us inside
from my own one-time balcony,
peeling tar paper and pooling water
now, closed the white-wood door
to a room I told you I kissed my own
first in, its edges littered
with dried bodies of bugs collected there,

you nodded at someone not there; I wondered
if the room was the sum of the paperlight
shells of its invaders and guests, summer
after summer, bloodless outlines,
if there was a heat that idled somewhere
that could stir their wings,
reanimate their legs to a scratch, a song, a symphony,
which one of us would hear it.

The Rockabilly Queen of Alaska

Wanda Thorpe can take a punch. Everyone knows that. Everyone knows she once slapped a woman right across the face with a little baby halibut—some say, but more likely a flounder—it was enough to splash the headlines in every *Otter Cove Times-Picayune* that lined the tables at J.R.'s diner, coffee rings by the end of the day circling in on Wanda and Rita Hickock, both booked, Wanda owed Rita something or other and refused to pony up, it spiraled from there, Rita's crooked mugshot nose harder to conceal in print than Wanda's missing molar, knocked from her face when we were growing up for trying to steal Missy Wheeler's boyfriend, brown curls spilling off the porch and out onto the dirt, flat on her back, blood filling her mouth like a hot bloom, flooding her barely ripe body. She whistles through it like a lullabye on windy days, tasting the nerve pain like homesickness.

She's sliced her fingers so many times her hands stopped swelling. She shuffles her feet in knee-high waders as she saws open the belly of each fish, cuts out the filets and the cheeks and the collars, slides their carcasses off the dock. She shuffles them in time to songs with names like "Crying" or "Squeeze Me Just a Little" or "In the Middle of a Heartache." She scrapes the scales off her knife and it looks like scraping the shine off the moon and dumping it right into the ocean. She likes to think she sees them all shimmering on the surface still, each scale; each body she lays hands on, leaves a little lighter than before; each song she touches the shivering heart of. But everyone knows, or should, that used-up flesh and sound can't float forever; it's really just the translucent bodies of jellyfish, reflecting what little light there is, a quiet sting dissolved by morning. Wanda knows it. She won a Wanda Jackson look-alike contest once. She pinned her hair just-so to match the long-gone queen of hillbilly music, but all the same, that her name was already Wanda didn't escape her.

What grows in winter? Everything here. Nothing shrinks from the salt, the wind, or the freeze; nothing sheds its old self or begins again under the doting warmth of a summer day. It's all one long day to an evergreen; rocks only gain more barnacles. Nothing forgets, and nothing backs down. Not Wanda, remembering Brendan Markham's fingers unspooling all her dreams onto her father's front lawn among the engine parts and broken reels, illuminating the dead and the stalled and the rusted with a cast-off light like the ever-burning neon of a distant city until they almost seemed to dance, and seeing him and Missy kissing on his front porch the very next day like electric eels up her spine, a sting that scorched her insides, a sting she knew would be worse to live with than any blow. Not Rita Hickock with what she felt the world owed her. Not anyone. There is no new heartache under the Otter Cove sun. When she heard "Everybody Loves Me But You" on vinyl, Wanda knew she was living a story that had been told before.

Say you're Wanda on a Saturday night. What do you do? Maybe Duane Eddy has the answer. "Because They're Young," and because you are too, still, you could argue, maybe you can still go out and make rust dance when you paint it on your lips and let them speak for you, still lose yourself in a place you've walked a million paces though, digging your ruts right into town. "You Can't Have My Love," you'll tell them, and they won't know which

Wanda is which, which is good, because between the Wanda who sings about how she's gonna rock it up and rip it up and how it doesn't matter anymore, and the Wanda whose hand trembles with need around her glass, it's good to have a little confusion. Or maybe Jerry Lee Lewis will walk you through how this night goes; "She Still Comes Around (To Love What's Left of Me)," so maybe you put ice packs on someone's split lip, knowing but not asking and not caring who started what, everyone started everything a long time ago, cooling a fever for a night that you can only really ever starve to death. Maybe when the throbbing subsides you slip into the ocean together at the edge of the world, emerge with lashes on your legs, a quiet sting dissolved by morning when you're lying awake feeling your own warm breath underneath your sheets as if someone else had never been there.

Billie Golden

[found poetry from obituaries and wedding stories from
The Washington Post]

Billie Golden died
on May 29, 1927.
Born May 29, 1927,
Billie Golden was 0 years old.

I learned an awful lot from him as a young kid.

It was a summer of long,
unstructured hours,
sometimes from game to game,
sometimes from period to period.

We'd write in chalk on streets and sidewalks
what became an immortal graffito
as the sun sank behind the Blue Ridge Mountains:
Will you take my hand
on an adventure?
PS I love you

Jerald Golden didn't sleep much
that week.
He worked construction in Alaska
from Brooks Range in the north to Bethel,
and south to the Gulf Range,
but now he worked his way to the stage.
His smooth voice,
preceded in death by his son,
was made husky by laryngitis.
They were living in separate cities;
the two hadn't said their final goodbyes.

A rush of electric tension grew.
A country band, Mother's Worry,
played throughout Kansas,
then Sparks, Nevada,
then Bay Minette (Alaska).

Back in Virginia, we'd been relayed the word
that Jerald joined his first, and last,
musical group that day—that day was now,

and each day following,
as we told and retold it,
put his words to different tunes
like "Yellow Rose of Texas"
or the slower, sweeter,
"My One and Only,"
or sometimes whispered it
in Jerald's shy croak:

Billie Golden died
on May 29, 1927.
Born May 29, 1927,
Billie Golden was 0 years old.

It was a long, unstructured
summer of hours.
We'd write in chalk on streets and sidewalks
what became an immortal graffito
as the sun sank behind the Blue Ridge Mountains:
Love is what turns pulse to song.

Murder Ballads

We take our hands from our clean, pressed shirts,
wrap them around a neck
and squeeze until the strings sing
to us. We need to bury our love
in shallow beds, lay down deep
beneath the ground, put a shotgun
to the temple of our grief.

It's our small flash of grace
that even as a crippling wind
moves the fields we walk through,
we bend a story with that same breath,
call out the secret
words for everything as we name them:
my mouth is a grave,
my tongue a tree split by lightning, a tuning fork,
and death is not a harvest waltz,
a scepter keeping perfect time
with a waxing moon,
but a flat-footed shuffle,
drunken and uneven, you can't help but follow
across the floor, a caller laying bare
the steps to a dance your body's been learning
since you could walk,
cooing to a packed room, "There is nothing
to this. Just move your feet."

Indian Summer

Yesterday
we knew where we stood,
buried in the feathers of our borrowed jackets,
wool grafted to our shoulders
in calculation of a predictable season—
brittle, bare, boundlessly
hungry.

Today, through the sunshine,
dread drips down like honey,
a dream where someone is talking backwards,
a mirror covered in fear
that someone or something
supposed to have left us
might glint back.

A shiva without a body.

We can't shake the feeling
that this is not ours,
that we were never meant to belong
in this place.
Nothing grows here,
though the light
calls and calls.
We compel ourselves to answer,
brittle, bare,
boundlessly hungry.

Aquagirl

I often wonder if all my motivation / is really my body knowing
secretly it's dying. / I'm always afraid to ask / or to listen too
closely.

But what else makes sense? / Lightning drawing to you
afternoon after afternoon / every summer / doesn't make you
unlucky / it makes you / a lightning rod / all your atoms hot
and ready / rushing through the high grassland of hairs
on the back of your neck / like a menacing wind.

I sometimes wish I could take two sips of whiskey / and slip
soundlessly into the creek / before the rain starts.

I've long suspected / I might be Aquagirl / a violet-eyed child
with strange nightmares / of a home she doesn't know
she was sent away from. / Night after night I dream
of being pulled away in a riptide / or drowned in a pool / or trapped
inside a washing machine / in a violent silent movie
my head pounding / into the sea floor / my chest ripping
down the middle / trying to seal itself / trying to preserve
dead oxygen / trying not to let
what's out there in—

until I open my mouth—let the water flood me—

breathe—

Epigenetics

You who are ever vigilant
of the danger that crawls and harvests
faster than you can: you tell me
Bacillus thuringiensis can be used to make kefir,
yogurt, cheese, and tiny parasites that kill
the caterpillars getting fat off the sweat of your hands,
your crop, day by day in which more succumbs
that you can't recover.

So trim and tend and then let the loam lay,
because that's the way
this is—part command, part plea,
presuming we've learned a part of the language
when anything on the earth responds.

And as the buds flower
and your homespun pesticide falls away
with the leaves, the crop retains a secret protection,
the same way climate change or diet can express
or silence genomes while the DNA looks the same—
inherited, and inherited, and lurking unseeable—
the way children of torture survivors
detect a sourceless, codeless trauma
living beneath their skin.

How much sorrow is born in our blood,
and how much kindness has been born of long-ago trout
we witnessed swung on a line like a lasso
by our younger brothers,
mouths gaping, afraid?
What fire were our great-grandparents under
that sweats us cold at night?
Whose hunger pains bore into our guts?

Who owns what here?
We graft and clone,
buy each other drinks,
circulate currency,
try to trade one bone ache for another,
to sieve out the poisoned marrow
from each other until we can't tell
where life began for one of us
and the strain ends for another.

But we are, in the end, made of pieces
unlendable. We learn to live
with our lungs. Just have to breath
through the bellow and collapse.

Marrow

You scrape the marrow from the bone
with a spoon and it looks like skimming moon-fat
off the skin of the ocean. You never knew it those sleepless nights

you'd wade down into it but it was nothing
you could have carried, just a reflection
of the jellyfish shimmering thanklessly

beneath the surface. Just photons and light
and a quiet sting you couldn't place,
dissolved by morning.

This is the soft codex of life, the inbred instructions
for assembling oneself over and over, no matter how
many parts are devoured or scraped away.

A bomb could burn through
a place you walked away from,
and no matter how close you draw someone

to you, how fervently the hair on their skin seems to rise
to your palms, only atoms will remember
the bodies they have made in this place.

Rivers

We go to them, twist our toes
into mossy blooms to anchor ourselves
against the rush that will be
the cold codex of an answer
that will come to us with our heads dunked
underwater, the waves of our shuddering
lungs and our shouting released
and whisked downstream and away
where our sound is not,
to echo more evenly across the water
later, on docks with beers and the stars
of tiny towns still lit upstream that we say look like galaxies,
shrinking ourselves, hoping
that our distance and our smallness will swallow us
and we'll be spit out clean in the morning
with mountain springs for veins.

Most of the time—

but most of the time,
two hikers come and squat
on a ridge eating breakfast burritos above us
and we swim in quiet, inoffensive circles
trying to keep them at our backs and act natural
as waterfowl without feeling like wildlife
being watched,
or we let our beers slip from our fingers,
lower them gently and release
them and they're the ones that swallow
water and their insides turn
brackish with a glug, glug, and we don't hear
them hit the bottom needlessly

as the idling high beams
that don’t belong to a squad car, after all,
pull away and fade, another pair of stars
in the sober, soundless night it was before
and we leave them there, and we’re left there,
knowing nothing
more of scale for losing them.

Thor's Well

We heard it before we could see it.
We had known that it would be difficult
to find, unmarked on maps,
unnoted by signs,
following folk trails on internet forums.

We should have known
our compass would be the sound
of a giant hammer as the tides broke
against the jetty,
spilled over and were sucked away
in illusion of the ocean being drained
into a giant hole within itself.

I followed its echo when you stayed
on the ridge and I climbed down to it,
and it retreated
from my sight as I got closer
until my toes curled
nearly at its edge.

Driving away, pulling a dog nose
close to my ear in the heat
of the car, I wonder now if I'm the same
as the one I was: she who once smoked cigarettes
in the corn with no signal,
halfway from home to home,
imagining lives unspooling in backseats
with each headlight as they moved
away from me and I moved
from every place;

wonder if the negative
space in skies and distances
drowns out old longings
ringing in our ears,
or just becomes more
hazy calls for us to divine,
multiplying the longer we look;

wonder whether it's the miles
or a willingness to run out of gas,
have your truck lifted by a tornado,
be swept into the ocean,
none of which I've ever had to prove
I would accept as consequence.

Out there, night had moved quicker than our feet.
Quickly I faded, until you couldn't see
the white of my hood,
the outline of my body,
whether I was still
standing at the edge
of a furious mouth that swallows feet
and births great whites, whales,
the bodies of seals that wash up
on the beach like deflated footballs.

Soon all we could hear
was the pounding of a hammer
on the rocks, which sounds a lot
like falling into the sea.

Backtracking

The women are upstairs
keeping an eye and coating macaroni,
smoothing the little hairs that rise up in summer
and curl like fiddleheads;
outside the air hisses with pipe smoke,
firecrackers, run-off fat disappearing
on glowing hickory, things I'd singe my hand on
later, things that keep the bugs away,
and wolves, I imagine, why we draw close
to it even with our hot hand gripping
a bag of frozen green beans,
but I'm neither place just then, I'm in the basement
with its mossy carpet and old-growth books,
pulling the same one down with each visit
to this house that isn't mine,
the textile cover bearing a cowboy
leaning on a cactus, a hat pulled low
across the eyes, the weight of a loneliness
I don't have language for
yet. I draw to it,
want to hold forever
that aching hole in my gut.
        But that was then;
every wound closes, and we trace the scars
like constellations of stories
to tell ourselves the rest of our lives.
Language is all I have of it now,
the way I say it, the way I graph that first feeling
into maps, the expanse of a life
built and corroded by what I think I remember:

that there was a story—one I couldn't read,
but whose shrouded cowboy told me wordlessly
that everything around us is too big for us to hold
but pieces of, for us to live in any way
but frame by frame, that it's big enough to swallow us,
but to let ourselves be swallowed is a kind of communion,
his bent body singing to me
the intimacy of lonesomeness,
the conversation of our living with the world—
and it's the only one that matters.

I slide the frames around.

I follow myself to a far coast, and when that isn't far
enough, north to a salt-licked frontier,
hang yellow curtains in a kitchen far from me now,
hold a home's bright light like a distant star.
Walk the shores of Sitka spruce
only when the rest have decided
it's safer not to. Want a fire
for its memory of the first air of autumn,
of the sweet smoke of a sweater,
of cold hands and hearts knocking
against a chain link fence.
Want to place a bag of frozen beans against
someone's skin still forming stories,
wondering which ones they've inherited
from me, which ones I can heal up.

Far from telephone poles,
it must be my own tracks calling me
back, rattling through the ground,

though I can't be certain
even in the perma-twilight if they're mine
or someone else's, here away from rising heat,
or where they tell me to keep walking
home to.

About the Author

Shenan Hahn is a writer and artist based in the Blue Ridge Mountains of Virginia, having returned home after a five-year sojourn in Oregon and Alaska. Her work has appeared in a wide variety of publications both online and in print, including *The Baltimore Review, Apeiron Review, Softblow, Lines + Stars, The Inflectionist Review, Rust + Moth,* and *Riggwelter*. She is the author of *In the Wake* (White Violet Press, 2014, under the name Shenan Prestwich), a full-length collection of poetry. She is a 2010 graduate of Johns Hopkins University's MA in Writing program, and has served in an editorial capacity for publications such as *Outside In Literary and Travel Magazine, Prompt & Circumstance,* and *VoiceCatcher.* Outside of her literary pursuits, she runs a small-town breakfast restaurant with her partner and enjoys long drives, old music, and blank canvases.

www.ingramcontent.com/pod-product-compliance
Lightning Source LLC
LaVergne TN
LVHW051022080826
845145LV00009B/2762

* 9 7 8 1 6 3 9 8 0 1 0 4 6 *